FLIPPING HOUSES FOR

BEGINNERS &

DUMMIES

BUY, FIX AND FLIP RESIDENTIAL PROPERTIES
(REAL ESTATE GUIDE)

BY: GLENN NORA

Table of Contents

Introduction

Flipping a home for profit can be an extremely lucrative endeavor, but only if you know how to go about it in the right way! That's what you will be able to do after reading this book. This book will provide you with all of the information that you'll need to get started flipping houses.

You have probably heard about flipping houses and have even given thought to the process and wondered whether you could get involved in this kind of investment. The truth is that if you are willing to put in the homework and learn what it takes to do it, and have the money to invest, you can!

Using the tips contained within the book, you can get on the road to success, but you need to be ready to take your investment very seriously. This book shows you how to take the various steps to ensuring that you are not only investing in property, but that you are able to make money at the end of your investment.

Hard work and a lot of good marketing can help you to get on your way to making a fortune as well as satisfying the demands of the market. When you have renovated and sold your first home for a profit, believe me, you will be on the "flipping" chain and nothing will stop you from doing the same thing all over again.

Taking the time to read through the following strategies and concepts on flipping houses will be your first exercise in gaining that knowledge and applying that patience. Then, you can enter the investment market with a firm foundation of skills, knowledge, and resources that will position you for success.

Chapter 1: Understanding House Flipping

What is house flipping

House flipping usually means that after repairs or improvements are made, the house is purchased and resold for profit.

Overall, it means buying a home that is going to be profitable and resold soon. This is a popular activity in the hot real estate market, especially among professional real estate brokers.

This is a quick profit strategy where investors buy real estate at discounted prices and improve real estate to sell at higher prices. If the housing market is strong, this is a very profitable strategy.

Old homes and mortgages are popular properties used in overturning homes because investors can get these properties fairly cheaply, increasing potential profits. In some cases, contractors are used to doing real estate upgrades, but experienced house flippers may do the work themselves.

Put simply, house flipping or flipping houses is making a business of buying a run-down house, renovating it, and then reselling it for a profit. Your foremost priority is deciding where to buy a house that will gain you the most profit.

The best place to scout for these types of houses is in foreclosed-home sales. With a little diligence, you could also find some cheap houses from real estate listings. You should always be cautious, however, because your money may go down the drain if you choose a house that cannot sell at a higher price quickly after you've invested time and money to renovate it.

The Essential Requirements

Up-to-date real estate information.

Reliable information about your target property and the community around it will help you arrive at sound decisions. Ensuring that the property is located at a strategic area near important institutions such as schools, hospitals, recreational places and malls is a prerequisite. The cost of the house is also something you must consider. Will you be able to resell it at a price high enough to recover whatever expenditures you incur, plus profit?

Sufficient cash

You'll need enough cash for the required down payment, and for the improvement, renovation or remodeling of the house. In addition, you may require cash for other miscellaneous expenses. The amount of cash that must be at your disposal will depend upon the cash value of the house you plan to buy.

Time

House-flipping takes time. Though it is a relatively quick process (ideally), you have to find time to get the house, fix the house, and then sell the house. If you have a full-time job already, this means filling your free time and weekends with the flipping project. If you don't have time and cannot make time for a house flip, you shouldn't do it. The longer you take to get the house ready and sold, the more money it costs you.

Money

Speaking of money, this is the second essential. Even if you are able to buy a house wholesale and pay less than you would otherwise on your flip house, you need money for repairs, taxes, and so on. Experts recommend a cushion, so you have a bit more flexibility when unexpected expenses pop up.

Knowledge

When you flip a house, you need to know what you're doing. This includes an understanding of the real estate market, house ownership, taxes, and construction. You can accumulate knowledge through reading, talking to people, and firsthand experience with making repairs, owning a home, and so on.

Ability to problem-solve

Being able to problem-solve is hugely important when you are flipping a house. It is inevitable that something will not go the way as planned, and you will need to figure out a new plan. An inspector might discover a problem that takes longer to fix than anticipated or a contractor might not work out and you have to find one on short notice.

Patience

It might take a while to find the perfect house to flip. Don't just buy whatever you see first and what costs the least amount of money. Those extremely cheap houses typically require a ton of repairs, which means more money and a longer construction time. Once you have the house you want, never sacrifice quality for a quick turnaround.

Good credit standing

A good or excellent credit score will be handy in case there is a need for additional cash. On top of the house renovations, there are other expenses that you will have to shoulder and prepare for; there are also realtor's fees and other contingency expenses to consider.

Ready market

As you begin the process of flipping a house, it helps if you already have a certain "type" of prospective buyer in mind. In any case, refrain from giving a house tour, however, until all renovation work is completed because the construction clutter will decrease the impact of your presentation. This will make it difficult to quote a good price to your buyer later on after the project is complete.

A team of experts

If you're new to flipping houses, you will learn that hiring professionals will be costly. In cases like this, you have the option to research on your own and do the homework that other experts would normally be called in for. If you can spare the time, you can enroll in affordable online courses and save on professional fees by being your own home inspector, appraiser, realtor, interior decorator, architect, or accountant. Doing some, or all, of these things for your house is a cost-saving measure.

An entrepreneur's persona

Excellent house flippers tend to possess these three specific personality traits: patience, diligence and flexibility. Flipping houses requires hard work, especially during the first few transactions. You have to be patient and diligent in doing research in order to avoid losing money, and more importantly, increase profits. Also, you'll need to be flexible in so far as having an ability to change your "game plan" during the purchase or sales phases if need be, since it's not unusual for real estate transactions to go not-as-planned.

Advantages of House-Flipping

You can make a quick profit

In only a matter of months, you can get your hands on a house, fix it up, and sell it for a pretty profit. This is especially true of buying wholesale, where you put the house under contract and then assign the contract to someone else. This person is the end buyer, and is responsible for the closing deal and associated costs. This means you can start flipping without a lot of money, and can have everything wrapped up in 6 months or less.

You meet a lot of people in the business

Networking is crucial if you want to get anywhere in the real estate business. By flipping houses, you meet a wide variety of professionals like realtors, inspectors, brokers, investors, and contractors. These people can become valuable partners in future projects, whether or not you choose to continue flipping houses or move into something else.

You learn a lot

You can't put a price on knowledge and experience, so whether or not your first house-flip is a smashing success, you walk away having learned about everything from finding a good deal, what to focus on in terms of repairs, and so much more. This knowledge and experience will serve you well when you decide to take on another flipping project, and allows you to make better decisions.

You get to be your own boss

One of the reasons people go into house-flipping - and even try to make it their full-time job - is because they get to be their own boss. This means you have total creative control over your project, you get to set your own hours, and you can learn from your mistakes without worrying about getting fired. This last benefit is very valuable in a house-flipping scenario, because your first-time flip will likely succumb to some mishaps and unpleasant surprises.

Real estate is a solid investment

The real estate market has changed over the years, but people always need houses, and if you're smart about things like location and getting a good deal initially, people will want to buy the house. There is inherent risk in any investment, but unlike playing the stocks where things can change at the drop of a hat, real estate is relatively stable and you are in control of a lot of the factors that impact profit.

Disadvantages of House Flipping

If house flips are profitable, the tax will be higher

"Flipping" is a term that refers to selling a house before closing it, basically by having someone pay to assign a purchase contract. However, most people use this term more commonly to refer to buying a home and reselling it at a higher price. You can make some money when it works, but tipping comes at a cost.

You don't always make a profit

There are a lot of ways you can lose money when you flip a house. From unexpected expenses related to construction to losing the profit you made on taxes, it is very easy to look at the numbers and realize you actually lost money when you took on the project. For many people, this can be a devastating loss and makes what you thought would be a cool way to earn some cash into a cash nightmare.

You can't always sell the house right away

Selling a flipped house is "supposed" to be the easy part, but too often it's the hardest step. Because you have to pay holding costs on the property you flip, not selling the house can gnaw away at your cash. You might even have to reduce the selling price, which makes any profit you make smaller. Not selling is also very frustrating because there's not much you can do besides wait.

Any mistake can have a huge impact

Another major disadvantage with house-flipping is that even a small mistake along the way can have huge consequences. Overlooking a repair or not choosing a good inspector can delay the resell process, and as mentioned in the paragraph above, the longer it takes for the house to sell, the more money gets drained away.

You can't pick up and run when things go bad

Although playing the stock market is riskier than the real estate business, you can always choose to move your money somewhere else. However, with house-flipping, you have to stick with a project until it sells if you don't want to hold on to it forever and lose money. You don't have many exit routes if things go south, so it is important to be really committed to seeing a project all the way through.

House-flipping can be more stress than its worth

House-flipping can be very stressful. From haggling deals to the physical labor of construction, both your mind and body can quickly get worn down by the process. This stress can affect your mood and family life in a negative way. Even if your house flip goes well, you might find yourself exhausted afterwards and realizing that the money just wasn't worth all the blood, sweat, and tears you poured into the project.

Do your research

Depending on where you look, you will find scores of other benefits and risks to house-flipping. When you're making your own list, do a lot of research so you can learn about all the possible rewards and risks. Talk to people who have flipped houses before or who have worked with people who have flipped houses. Ask them what they would have done differently if they could go back in time, and also about what they would do again. Educating yourself is the first and arguably the best thing you can do when you're deciding whether house-flipping is a good idea.

Determine the Market Value

Before getting into the whole business of flipping houses, you need to know one very important factor that will determine your success or failure in this field: market value.

Several factors affect market value. These are location, surrounding neighborhood, and amenities. Location means the physical placement of the property where it's at. If the property is near a city, or within the city limits, it has a higher value than a house in the middle of nowhere. Surrounding neighborhood means the people who are living within the area are there noisy neighbors, is crime-rate low, are there families with children. Amenities refer to conveniences residents enjoy within the said area like schools, clubhouses, pools, golf courses, *etc.* All of these factors affect how high or low you can sell your flipped house. Market value dictates the ceiling price, and from there, you can estimate your total investment, and the profit you can get.

Chapter 2: Who You Need on Your Team

An important aspect of acquiring homes to flip, especially if you're planning on doing this frequently, requires forming relationships with reputable people in a variety of industries. You don't want to be working with people who are trying to swindle you or whom you do not intimately know. Let's take a look at some of the relationships you're going to want to cultivate as you become increasingly proficient in the processes of house flipping.

A General Contractor

If your current day-job is the role of a professional contractor, then you are well ahead of many other house flippers out there. If you're not a professional contractor, all is not lost; however, you're going to want to find someone who you can trust and who can provide you with good results. In case you're unaware, a general contractor is someone who you can count on to provide your home with the materials and labor that is involved in any given construction project that you may need completed.

A Certified Public Accountant (CPA)

As you probably already know, property investors are able to reap the benefits of certain tax benefits when the time comes to pay taxes on an investment property. Of course, in order to cash out on these tax benefits that the government offers, you have to know how to do your taxes properly. This is why you should be motivated to find a CPA who specializes in investment property-related endeavors. These people definitely exist and should not be too difficult to find, especially because of the fact that property investing is a growing and lucrative business.

Realtor

Your realtor should be able to get the house that you want for the price you want but also sell the house that you have created for the price that you want to sell it for. This is something that they need to be able to do and finding the right one can make a huge difference in your investment property.

It is always a good idea to find a realtor who has a great reputation and one who has worked with investors in the past because they will know how to handle your situation in the best way possible.

Inspectors

It is a good idea to have the inspection done well in advance of the open house in case anything comes up with the property or you need to change something that is not up to code. Your inspector will be able to tell you what needs to be changed, if anything, long before you are set to show the home to potential buyers. The inspector should also be there before your final inspection with the city.

Stagers

Stagers are people that will come into your home and will set up furniture, tchotchkes, and other décor that will make the newly renovated home look like it is lived in. They are experts in design, and many of them were interior designers before they began staging homes. They have many pieces that they can put into your home and the right stager will know just what to do for your home. From using neutral tones to baking cookies before the open houses, the stagers can set the mood for selling the home. Help your stager out, and he or she will help you. Remember, staging is sometimes the single thing that sells your home's

A Lending Source

Flipping a property is no cheap endeavor. This is even more true when you're new to the flipping housing market and do not have any other properties that are bringing you capital. This is why establishing a good working relationship with your lending source is all the more important when you're new. Whichever method you end up using to obtain the funds, it's important to find a lending institution who can be held accountable and is also trustworthy. Finding a lender who possesses these two qualities is extremely important, especially if you are planning to make flipping properties a long-term career for yourself. Who knows, if things work out smoothly with your lender, they could even end up approaching you about investing in another venture later down the line. When you have a good working relationship with someone who has a steady stream of money, more things are possible.

A Landscaper

You may not think about the cost of hiring to maintain a home's lawn as being a big expense, but what happens if a tree falls down, or you need to remove an old tree that is starting to rot? These are the types of situations that you need to be prepared for as both a potential landlord and property flipper.

Chapter 3: Financing your House Flipping Venture

One does not necessarily need to have a big capital in order to start a business. With a little research and preparation, you can find ways and means to raise funding for a new venture. The meticulous effort you put into creating your business plan will now bear fruit as you present the plan to people who can help fund your house flipping business. Listed below are the possible financing sources you can consider:

Business partners

A business partner, who will provide funding while you do the legwork and the flipping tasks, is a viable option. Both you and your partner can earn from your investments. He or she invests money, and you invest your time and effort. Create proper legal contracts to document every detail of your agreement and partnership to prevent potential legal issues later on.

Banks or lending companies

You can take out a bank loan as starting capital for your house flipping business. You have to earn more than what the bank demands as interest for your loan. Opt for moneylenders who give you the lowest interest rating and those with flexible payment options.

Investors

Search for willing investors for your business. Your first investors may be your friends or family members, who trust you enough to invest. Gradually, as your business progresses, more and more investors will come to your assistance. Your good integrity as a house flipper will surely increase the number of your investors.

Personal savings

Another way to raise business capital is to save for it. You can use existing savings but be aware of the risks that are involved in doing so.

Government grants or loans

Inquire from your local or state government if there are grants and loans for small entrepreneurs or business owners like you. Prepare your Business Plan and Business Proposal for presentation. These plans have to outline clearly what you intend to do and achieve in your flipping business. Calculate how much interest you'll pay and compare it with your projected income from flipping a house. Government grants typically charge smaller interest rates than banks and lending companies so we recommend choosing this option if a grant is available.

Second mortgages

You can only avail of this type of funding if you don't have any options left. Before doing this, determine the equity of your home. If the equity is almost negative, look for other options of obtaining money. Since you're using a second mortgage, most likely, your house will serve as the collateral. Hence, when something goes wrong with your flipping business, you lose your house. Becoming homeless is not your goal. Use a second mortgage only when you're certain you can cover the scheduled payments. Nevertheless, risking big things to obtain bigger things is sometimes necessary in order to succeed. Go for it if you deem the risk is worth it.

Raise money

As a house flipper, you have to learn how to raise money for your next flip. Showing people how much they can earn as potential investors by helping you raise money is the general idea. Don't ask for money. Let them voluntarily contribute their cash for your goal. Don't promise big earnings however. Explain to them comprehensively how flipping houses works so they can understand that their earnings are dependent on how successful your house flip is. They can act as secondary or primary investors with percentage earnings depending on the amount they invest.

Sellers

You can partner with a seller to flip a house, and then later on share in the proceeds of the business. He can also choose to be a silent partner and invest funds only, if he doesn't want any of the action.

Buyers

The same principle applies to your potential buyers of the renovated house; they can serve as partners or investors.

All of your agreements should have documents or contracts duly prepared by a licensed attorney to legalize the agreement. The details must be clearly stated and witnessed. Having a lawyer attend to the legal nitty-gritty will ensure that everything is done in accordance with the law.

Chapter 4: Finding a Flip-Worthy Home

Once you've thought through the essentials and specifics that you need, it's time to start looking at houses. Remember, if you aren't sure about a property, don't risk it. Be extra careful for your first flip and seek advice from those more experienced than you. It is ultimately your decision however, and if you feel confident that you have thought through everything you need to, go for it.

Beginners spend a lot of time wondering and worrying whether they have found the right house to make a profitable flip or not. Let's put your mind to rest!

Apply Your Flipping Formula

Setting the Current Market Value

Once you have located a home that peaks your interest, go on Zillow to find homes that have sold in the neighborhood. If possible, go no further back than the past six months. Also, try to stay within a few blocks radius of the house you intend to flip. If you need to expand your search area, go out no further than one mile. In a perfect world, you should be able to find several houses that have sold in the past two to five months within the area.

Figuring the Costs of Estimated Repairs

Estimating costs might be tough because some issues will be hidden and crop up later as ugly surprises. Getting estimates and feedback from your construction people is critical, especially for beginner flippers. After you've been in the business for a while, you get good at eyeballing things, but at first, you'll want to rely on the professionals to give you accurate figures.

Figuring the Value of the Home after Refurbishing

Using the same area as you did when finding the current market value, look at the homes that are for sale. Find out what they are selling for, and compare them with the home you are flipping. In a perfect world, after the repairs are made, and the house looks incredible, how does yours compare with the others? Knowing what other homes are selling for will not increase the real value of your flip, but it will let you know what buyers will see as they shop for a new home. If you were a buyer, which home would you prefer to purchase, and why? This is particularly the case for upper-end homes, because your customers are somewhat limited and you'll be vying for the same people.

Where to look for houses

Real estate agents

Armed with a list of requirements such as two bedrooms, must cost under $300,000, and so on, a real estate broker can locate properties that match what the client wants. Their weapon is the multiple listing service (MLS), a database brokers use to find houses for clients.

Real estate groups

A real estate group, or club, consists of a bunch of investors and professionals such as contractors, brokers, accountants, and so on. Together, they talk about their projects and share knowledge. This is a great place to make connections and hear about any available listings that might make for the perfect flip.

Probate house sales

These probate sales are good sources of houses to flip because their properties are offered at affordable, discounted prices. Sometimes the people concerned would like to see their inherited properties converted into cash as soon as possible, and that's where you can come in.

Online listings of individual sellers

There are online users who are in dire need of money and are selling their houses as direct sellers to whoever may be interested. This transaction will eliminate the fees for real estate brokers, which is an advantage for you. This listing may be posted on the person's blog, website or social sites of which he or she is a member.

Property Wholesalers

Wholesalers of houses are great sources of houses to flip. They can also offer cheaper prices for the houses overall. All you need to do is to find out who the wholesalers are within your area.

Multiple Listing Service (MLS)

There are many different MLS websites. Some of my favorites include ZipRealty.com and TheMLS.com. You can do an advance search to specify the price ranges you can afford and the number of rooms or the other details that you want. From the results you can select the best house to flip. During the initial stages of step one, where you create your business plan, it is helpful to do a bit of research with MLS house listings to get an idea of the costs and estimates of property in a specific area.

Local newspaper

The leading local newspaper will surely have a list of houses on sale in your location. Choose from this list and do an ocular visit to determine the house's suitability for flipping.

Television

Television is a good source of houses for sale. Just be ready with your pen and paper to list down telephone numbers and addresses.

Tax auctions

When a homeowner can't pay their property tax, tax collectors will auction the unpaid tax. Usually, whoever bids the most cash gets the lien on the property in the form of a sheriff's deed. Houses for sale at tax auctions can be very cheap, but getting a house this way is also extremely risky.

Foreclosure listing websites

The Internet is a treasure trove of foreclosures. Sites like Foreclosure.com and RealtyTrac list are solid resources for finding affordable houses. Before you buy a house you find on the Internet, it is a good idea to check on the house using a site like BuildFax. For a fee, the site will give you the specs on the house's past repairs, remodels, and so on. This information can help you haggle for a lower price and identify which listings are accurate and which ones are claiming the house is worth more than it really is.

Chapter 5: Assessing a House

After selecting a property to purchase, the next step is to check the house itself. Once you're convinced that it will be a good project, buy it! After buying the house, start your publicity campaign. Keep in mind that the property is being renovated and it will be available for purchase soon. This will attract potential customers so that by the day of the open house, you will get a ton of offers.

Taking a Look at Houses

Structural problems

You may think that you are pretty good when it comes to decorating, though how good are you at looking at property beyond the surface? Any structural work to the house will cost you money, so that the first consideration should always look for items such as these:

- Rising damp

- Rotten wood

- Bowed walls

- Bad roofs

- Foundation problems

- Insect Infestation

- Faulty wiring

- Faulty plumbing

These are all serious considerations, as there are costly repairs. Unless you can ask the advice of an expert and get costs in very fast, don't touch houses that don't have solid foundations or have structural problems. No matter how much you make the house look nice on the inside, unless you tackle the structural problems, you are going to lose money. Avoid these like the plague. It's great if the house is built on a solid foundation, has great walls, no signs of dampness and floors that are flat. Look out for these and you won't go too far wrong.

Leaks

Leaks may appear on a ceiling and you can usually trace where the leak started. It may be that guttering needs to be replaced, or that a bathroom on a higher level hasn't got a great seal around the shower or bath. Leaks may also have gotten into the insulation within the wall space, so you need to use a damp meter as you won't actually know how much mold is in the wall until you strip it. A damp meter can give you an idea and that's better than no idea at all. If you do have to replace all the insulation, then that's extra expense.

Wear and tear

People don't like buying houses with bathrooms and kitchens that are dated and these areas give you a great idea about how well a home has been looked after. There could be all kinds of things hidden beneath the drywall that you didn't anticipate. Wear and tear is one thing, but actual neglect is another entirely and could cost you your entire contingency and thus eat into your profits.

Keeping notes of costs

Keeping note of potential costs helps to remind you of what you thought while you were going through the property and that's important because without those notes, you may actually forget something important.

As a new developer of property, there are certain things that you need to look out for when you are considering the purchase of a property.

Think about the investment value Rather than How nice the house appears to be

While you may think that's pretty obvious, it is surprising how many people forget that the marketability of the house at a profit is the main aim of flipping houses. It has to bear in mind several different factors. These include the market itself and how viable it is to propose a sale of a house in the current market. This takes a lot of study. If there are a glut of houses for sale in that geographical area at the time of purchasing, this is what's called "A Buyer's market" and that means that buyers have a wonderful choice of property and can almost dictate the price level at which a house will be sold. A seller's market is something entirely different. This is when there is a shortage of houses within that geographical area even though the amount of people looking for a home remains unchanged. That means that a house is more likely to gain a good price.

The second thing that needs to be borne in mind is the math. Take a look at this breakdown because you need to be able to think in terms of profit, rather than speculation.

House Value

You will need to do a lot of studying if you want to get the market just right. The best areas to look for properties that are foreclosed are those areas which are highly desirable – where there is an established reputation and demand. Occasionally, you find the odd house which is within that belt and you are able to not only do the work, but up the price to give you a wonderful profit, but you do need to study in advance. Since there are others in the same market as you, that means being very aware of your facts so that when that potential bargain comes up for sale, you are able to pull figures together quickly and make a good solid prediction of how much profit you can expect to make on the property.

You can guarantee that a house is put on the market at an optimistic rate. People want to make as much money as is possible. However, there are real pointers to whether you can put in a cheeky offer.

Chapter 6: Making an Offer

Now that you have found the home that you want to invest in, you have figured out that it is a great deal and you have secured the financing that you need to be able to purchase it, you may be eager to jump onto it as quickly as possible. That type of gusto will help you, but you also need some help to beat out the other competition on the home. Chances are, you won't have much time to make an offer to the seller.

Get Friendly

Remember, being friendly is only the first step toward making the seller choose you and getting the home that you want to be able to renovate. There are much more things that are involved but setting up the framework with a positive attitude, and a friendly demeanor will only help you. Even if you have the highest offer, the only place that will guarantee you a home is an auction. Be as likeable as possible so that the sellers will want to sell to you.

Stand Out

To help you stand out to the seller, ask them what their favorite part of the home is. Most people have a favorite part of their own home, and you can appeal to them by taking their feelings into account. If you have not seen that part of the home yet, ask them to show it to you so that you will be able to see their reaction to the favorite part. Try your best to see what they love so much about it and let them know that you understand why they like that area.

Don't Take Too Long

Once you have made an offer on a home, you have 15 days to get someone to inspect the home before you make the decision on whether you truly want to buy it. This gives you the assurance that you need to make the right choice for your home.

Try to bring your contractor or someone else who can inspect the property along with you to the showing of the home. He or she will be able to tell you what they think will need to be done and what you can expect after you have actually purchased the property.

Shoot High

The seller has set the price of the house for a reason. Either he or she has an emotional attachment to it or they think that it is truly worth the amount that they are asking. Don't offend the seller with a lowball offer. If you think that the home needs a lot of extra work, consider bringing that point up at the open house. The seller may be ignorant to that fact and may consider lowering the price. If you do not get anywhere by doing this, you need to just move on. Finding a different house will be a better option than trying to get the house for a very low price, offending the seller and making a bad name for yourself in the real estate community. You are trying to build up your home investment business, not tear it down when you are looking at your very first property.

You should make your offer based on the list price, and it really shouldn't be any lower than the list price. This is the price that you figured your budget up with, anyway, so it should not make a difference if you have to pay the full price for your house. Most of the time, if a seller gets a full price offer on the home that they are trying to sell, they will take it right away. Try to get your offer in before any of the other buyers who are trying to get the home, too. Your offer being the first could secure the home for you.

When you have seen a house, don't be too quick to make an offer without first assessing the potential cost to renovate the house and put it back onto the market. Sit down and work out the costings, the time period that it will take to do the works and how much you feel should be deducted due to the market value in the area at the time that you are buying. If you are too quick, you are showing too much keenness which will give the seller the impression that you are desperate.

Your offer should be an all-inclusive offer and sometimes you can even get the seller to include the payment of the real estate agent fees just because they want to get rid of the house. Take into mind the following:

- How long has the house been on the market?

- What will it cost to refurbish it?

- What price will you realize when you sell it? – Be realistic

- Decide upon what your potential profit margin is.

When you know your profit margin that gives you an idea of how much bartering you are prepared to do to get the house.

On the day that you make the offer, there should be no room for discussion. Make the offer, let the seller think about it and wait until the seller comes back to you, whether this is through a real estate agency or not. If you push for a decision, you show your hand as desperate to buy and the seller will ask for more. The waiting game is worth it. When the seller does come back to you, they will no doubt give a counter amount which means that they are not prepared to accept less than X amount of money. That doesn't mean that you have to pay that amount. It's just a picture of their expectation.

Go in again and offer somewhere between what the seller wants and what you have offered because there is still a chance that you can get the price reduced. It may sound like penny picking, you really need to be this fussy because it's a business you are running and you can't afford to throw cash away.

Once your offer is accepted, you can start to draw up plans of what you intend to do to the home and get your plans in action. If these plans include getting permits, then these can be applied for so that you save yourself time once you take ownership of the house. The plans include your schedule of works and drawing up a program so that you know exactly how long the work will take and can make sure that your finances meet the obligations that you will have as a result of the work being done.

Chapter 7: Real transformation Through Renovation

It is smart to work with a designer when doing renovation because a good designer can tell you what you need to do to add value to the house without really shelling out too much cash. However, hiring designers can be expensive.

Discussions with Contractors

You will need time to discuss items with contractors and you should make appointments within these days, but not rely upon one company for each trade. It's always a wise move to have several quotations to work with and have the contractor itemize the quotation so that you can compare like for like when making your decision. Make appointments to meet with contractors and space out the appointments so that you see each contractor at a different time. The real estate agent may just let you have the key if the house is unoccupied and you explain that you have many appointments with contractors. It's obvious that you are seriously considering the house, so the agent shouldn't mind too much.

Make a list of your repairs and make sure you have covered all of the repairs or potential repairs that you would not perform yourself. It may be a few days before you get the official word from the contractors, but make them aware that time is important especially if there is competition for purchasing the house.

Suggestions on how to go about renovation work in a smart and budget-safe way

Do a thorough walk-through of the house and make a list of everything you want to work on, both inside and out. Major fixes like new roofing are already on your radar because you needed to know how much money it would cost before you bought the property, so this list is more about keeping a record of the work for time's sake. Exterior fixes could include gutters, landscaping, doors, and painting. Even include the minor fixes like a new doorbell, house number, and so on. For the inside, look at wall patches, windows, door trims and hinges, electrical switches, bathroom and kitchen fixtures, and painting. When you are making your master repair list, arrange it according to importance. For example, replacing the old linoleum in the bathroom is more important than repainting the door trim.

This is the ideal opportunity to get rid of items that you no longer want in the house. Old carpets can be ripped up and the house can literally be gutted ready for the refurbishment. Perhaps you are replacing old flooring with new and modern flooring such as a quality laminate. These are very popular these days and give clean lines. Remove linoleum and trims which are damaged since these are relatively easy to replace and will give great crispness to the look of your house.

Taking one room at a time, remove all of the items that are no longer required. This includes old light fittings, furniture which was left by the previous owner and wall coverings if wallpaper is to be removed.

The point is that the cleaner the area is to work in, the quicker you can get on with cleaning up the house and fixing any areas of cracking, ready to coat up the walls with paint. At this stage, take a note of repairs that need to be completed in each room so that you are constantly aware of the work needing to be done.

With the bathrooms, since this is a flip, check if all the parts are in working condition or need replacements. It will be good if toilets, bathtubs, and the shower can be salvaged so that is one less expense you can spare. However, upgrading fixtures and installing a new vanity is good investment. Make sure to replace shower curtains and grout tiles thoroughly.

If you decide to redo the entire bathroom, make sure that you do all the bathrooms in the house, not just the master bath. Also, try to keep the changes uniform. If you get new counter tops for the master bath, choose the same slab for all the other bathrooms.

With the kitchen, check if the cabinets are still good and can be upgraded simply by re-staining. However, go new with the sink and install stainless steel. A new faucet will also be a good investment as well as nice countertops.

Adding new appliances in your kitchen will also add value to the house. Another thing that you can consider is adding a nice back-splash that not only compliment the kitchen, but ties all the color combinations together.

For the bedrooms, the more bedrooms, the higher the value. So, if you can turn a den into another bedroom, do it. Changes that can be done to a bedroom to make it appealing should be confined to the floor, ceiling, and walls unless there's damage in other places that render the room unusable. Give it a fresh coat of paint, redo the carpet, and replace light fixtures.

Closets are also good investments for flips. Customers like seeing upgraded closets with lots of space and pre-installed organizers.

Adding these items to a house where they are not present will not add value. It simply brings the property up to the standard level of the remaining houses in the neighborhood and allows you to charge a competitive price.

Also, you must ensure that your property stands out from all the competitors' properties. You must not make any unreasonable improvements that are extravagant as compared to other properties in the region. Not only will you lose money, but it will also scare off potential buyers too. In short, before you invest a lot of money in a complex full-house renovation project, you should consider what competing for real estate in your area could offer. Find out how similar properties in your area are valued and improve them according to your specific market.

If you are trying to make the property look more attractive, then now is not the time for any bold changes to the scenery. Instead, try to come up with quick fixes that will instantly improve the appeal of the house. Something as simple as adding a sheer accent wall or even chic back panels with simple designs can improve the way the house looks. Another element that you can change without burning a hole in your pocket is lighting. By changing the lights and opting for soothing and pleasant LED lamps and lights, you can make the house look bright and fresh. If you need any help with these home improvement projects, then you can always contact an interior designer. Just make sure that you don't go overboard with these expenses and stick to a predetermined budget. Quick fixes like changing the lighting and the lighting fixtures in the house not only make the house look attractive, but are cost effective too.

There's nothing wrong with adding these items to your home, of course, but do not expect potential buyers to pay a premium to get them when you are ready to sell. And be careful when updating means replacing a popular or regular feature. If there is a two-car garage in another house near you, you should probably not be considering turning your home into a playroom. Do you want to be the only home in the area without secure parking?

Plan on tackling the most important stuff first

It makes sense to do the big fixes first. You don't want to save the kitchen or bathroom for last, and then find out it will take longer than you planned. If you're running out of time and you just have minor fixes like updating doorknobs, it's much easier to rush through those and not have serious consequences. It's also in your best interest to work on the big stuff when you have all your money. Crucial fixes include anything broken, warped floors, any holes in anything, and so on.

Decide who will be doing the work

If you have been smart and kept track of your money, you will have a clear idea of the kinds of repairs you need and how much it will cost. Now comes the part where you decide if you want to do the repairs yourself, or if the work is outside of your skill set. If the repairs are really basic, you might not even need to hire a contractor.

Set deadlines and work schedules

Since flipping a house is intended to be a quick process, you will need to set a timeline for repairs. Ideally, you will have considered how long each repair will take *before* you bought the property, but now is when you need specific deadlines. What needs to be done in each room and how long do you think it will take? Be realistic, especially if you are not the one doing the hands-on work. It may be tempting in this case to hope for a very quick turnaround, but your contractor disagrees. Defer to the experts. If you are doing the work yourself, plan out when you can be at the house and write up a schedule along with what you want to work on during that time.

Clean everything

Even if you can't update everything like you want or change the paint color, you want to be sure that everything is thoroughly cleaned before any potential buyer comes through. Construction is a messy business, so clean up any sawdust and dust from all the rooms. Make sure the bathrooms and kitchen are sparkling clean, too, since most buyers will be looking at those spaces very carefully. You can even get professional cleaners to come in if it is in your budget. Don't forget the outside! Make sure the lawn is cut and sidewalks clear.

Cut the bushes. Simple pruning of overgrown shrubs can greatly enhance the attractiveness of the home. Sometimes getting rid of certain bushes when they start to look too wild can instantly beautify the property.

By simply mowing the lawn and watering it regularly, you can make it look healthy, vibrant, and attractive. A good-looking lawn improves the overall curb appeal of a property. Ensure that you weed and fertilize the lawn regularly. The lawn must not have any bare spots on it and if there are exposed areas then you need to fill them with new patches of grass.

Stick to Your Budget

This is probably where all the stress in flipping will come in. The budget you use for flipping should not push you into a corner where you'll be desperate to sell it and get it over with quick. To avoid this, set a budget and stick to it.

It is possible to follow a strict budget, and having a budget will keep you from over-improving the house as well. Remember, you're flipping the house to sell it, not live in it.

Chapter 8: Staging for a Quick Sale

Staging a house is the art of presenting your house flip to buyers as a warm, livable place for their family. This is especially important with flipped houses, because otherwise they would just be empty spaces with no real character. There are people who stage houses as their profession, but with some common sense, it is pretty easy to do it yourself. It is especially easy to do it with a flipped house, because you never lived there and don't have personal furniture or possessions to deal with.

Stage for Your Target Market

If your flip is in a retirement area, don't stage it with a nursery or toys in a children's room. Instead, include a study or reading room with a cozy throw over a rocking chair. If your flip is across from an elementary school, chances are your buyers will have younger children. If this is the case, then include a room with bunk beds and a small desk, or perhaps a shelf with some toys or sports items. If your flip is in a neighborhood with a lot of teens, maybe you would want to include a basketball hoop above the garage or to the side of the driveway. These items would enable the buyers to imagine themselves as owners.

Arrange neutral furniture in conversational settings

Avoid bright, overly-unique furniture. Instead, chose simple furniture in neutral colors like creams, beiges, and grays. You can get your own furniture, or, which is probably more convenient for a house flip, you can rent from a staging company. Arrange the furniture into "conversational" groups, which basically means how you would arrange furniture if you were having people over. You would want sofas away from the walls and facing each other. This will make the room seem more open and large, even if it is on the small side.

Give every room a function

Some house flips have weird rooms that no one knew what to do with, but you don't want any room of the house to seem bare or awkward. Assign a function to every room and decorate accordingly. A smaller room on the first floor could be an office or playroom.

Make the house warm and appealing

This means no smudged windows, rolled-up rugs, or power tools lying around. Stage the house like you're having company. If it is winter, have the heat on. Smell is one of the most sensitive senses, so make your guests feel at home by using fragrance diffusers, or even baking cookies or making coffee.

Give the house curb appeal

The first impression of any house is the outside. More people will drop in if they notice how good the house looks just by driving by. Make sure the grass is cut, the door is well-painted and clean, and the mailbox isn't falling apart. If it is in your budget, you can plant a garden or even add a water feature.

Minimize the Bad and Accentuate the Good

Every house has its ills, and your flip is sure to be no exception. What you can do with staging will surprise you. Get in the habit of writing down what first attracted you to your flip because chances are it is an appealing feature that you can accentuate to attract other buyers. For example, if your flip has an amazing fireplace, then center the furniture around the fireplace. Place some tall plants to the side or some beautiful accessories on the mantle to draw the buyer's eye to the house's high points. If the living room has a huge picture window, don't hide the window with heavy drapes. Instead, place the furniture in a manner that allows lots of light to shine through and gives the buyers full view of the front or back yard.

Adding Accessories

Pillows, throws, vases, trays, *etc.* can be added to your staging efforts to give the flip splashes of color, texture, and height. If you are staging an older home with low ceilings, don't use a lot of tall items that will draw attention to the fact that the ceilings are low and not very contemporary. When arranging accessories, there is magic in three. Three candlesticks of different heights or three pillows grouped together add balance.

Lighting is Everything

Lighting in a room can add warmth, cheer, and a welcoming feeling. Well-placed lamps and pendants will automatically draw the eye to the source of the light. Pulling the drapes and opening the blinds are a must, or just leaving everything off the windows is fine to maximize the light and open the room. Sometimes just a valance to add color and texture and draw the eye to a higher ceiling is all it takes to showcase positive features of the home.

The Challenges of Staging

If you have no place to store your staging furniture and accessories at home, then you'll need to rent a storage space. It can get expensive to store and move the furniture to stage homes, but studies have shown that staged homes sell quicker and for more money.

If you decide to stage your flips, purchase smaller pieces that are light and easy to move and place. You can always group them to create weight in a room, but you cannot take bulky furniture and fit it into a smaller home.

Chapter 9: Putting your Property in the Market

Marketing is the key part of selling a home. Even if you've done a great job on the renovation, the house is in a great location, and it has a reasonable asking price, no one will buy it if they don't know it exists.

Put an ad in the newspaper

This is an old-fashioned method, but it can still work, depending on the area and market. Get a newspaper and check to see if any comparable houses are advertising. In terms of readership, the Sunday edition of a newspaper probably has the biggest audience. You want to write a good home ad. Come with a snappy headline that describes the house or highlights the definitive quality of the home.

Neighborhood Blog

Most neighborhoods have a blog where people can advertise anything they have for sale, their businesses and services, and even a lost pet. The blog is also a good way to market your flip. Use the neighborhood blog and start far ahead of time so that you can encourage people to pay attention to the status of the improvements.

Put A "For Sale by Owner" Sign Out Front

If you put it in the MLS right away, put your brokerage sign out front and attract as many buyers as you can from the sign so that you can refer to another agent in your office and collect referral fees. You can also do this with a "For Sale by Owner" sign. You'll be receiving a lot of calls from interested buyers, and you can refer those as well. A simple way to get their number is to put them off for a moment.

Fliers

If you are putting signage out front, include your fliers or ads in a holder attached to the sign. Add more pictures than information. Don't answer all the buyer's questions on the posted flyer. You need to give them a reason to call. Be sure to make the phone number bigger and bolder on the flyer, so it's easy to find. If you are licensed, be sure to have the approval of your broker for all the information that needs appear in the fliers.

Neighborhood Yard Sale

If you want all the neighbors to see the home first, you ought to hold a neighborhood yard sale. Get as many neighbors involved as possible, put up a ton of signs advertising multiple family yard sale, and then put out your open house signs with advertisements for the furnishings as well. Make it a celebration with balloons, a cookout, and a lot of excitement and enthusiasm. Serve the neighbors lunch as they work their yard sales. Yard sales are a good time for potential buyers to tour the house and see how friendly and welcoming the neighbors are. Plus, it's a party atmosphere, and everybody loves a party.

Craigslist

As you advertise the yard sales, put it on Craigslist as well. You might want to post some pictures of the inside and outside of the house and then say there is a ten-family block yard sale, including free hotdogs and hamburgers, and everything must go, including the house. Prepare to have a lot of traffic through the house. It might be a good idea to put down some plastic in the high-traffic areas to protect the carpet. Or, set out that box of booties and encourage everyone to cover their shoes.

Local Retailers

If you have a few smaller strip centers near your flip, it's always fun to take a little glass container of chocolates with a picture of your flip wrapped around the jar. Ask if you can leave some flyers of the home as well, and be sure to ask for a few cards of theirs to pass out to all those who tour your home. Let them know they'll be able to hand-pick their customers.

Put an ad online

Writing an Internet ad is like writing a newspaper ad. With a site like Facebook, you can create a targeted ad that gets shown to people who live in a specific area, are in a certain age range, and more. Using your own Facebook page, you can "promote" your status for very little money.

Chapter 10: Time to Sell

There are a couple of different things that you must keep in mind when you think about selling the property. Including good photos along with good descriptions can make the difference between getting a good deal on a property and the property being left unsold.

Dressing the Property for Sale

The décor should be fairly neutral but warm enough for people to be able to envisage living in that home with the minimum of work. Avoid really dark colors. A pop of color here and there is much better in soft furnishings or vases because these can be changed easily by someone who buys the house, whereas wallpaper or paint in garish colors will mean extra expense for the potential buyers. That's bad news for you because they may also ask for a price reduction in order to get the house into the state they want it to be in ready to live in it.

Building your Reputation

As you begin to get more confidence, you need to build your reputation with many people. That includes the planning department, your workmen, your real estate agent and your potential clients. If you are in the business of selling homes then you also need to keep a record of people who have contacted you because although you may not have what they are looking for, the chances are that they do make a potential buyer of a future project. Just like real estate agents build their clientele register, you need to keep in touch with people that matter.

The Right Time

You have to make sure that you are selling the property at the right time. Real estate tends to be seasonal, and if you want to sell the flipped property quickly, then be sure that you are doing it at the right time. For instance, the ideal time to list a property for sale is between March and May since most property deals tend to be finalized during this time. The sales of properties tend to increase at the beginning of a new financial year instead of during or at the end of a financial year.

Right Description

The right words are just as important when it comes to selling your home. Share with potential buyers how impressive your home and the neighborhood are, including information on nearby schools, shopping, or regular activities offered near your home. Include information that showcases certain other fetching details about the property and the surrounding areas along with the basic information. The buyer needs to feel like they are looking at a special property.

Pricing

The price is one of the most important determinants of the sale of real estate. If the price is too high, you can end up spending much more time on the market than you would like. By researching and comparing other properties, you can see if your offer matches the rest of the market. However, compare similar properties in the environment to achieve a realistic price range.

Viewings

When you take people around the home, try to remember to keep the doors open so that the rooms have great flow. People don't like tripping over things or awkward entrances to rooms. Try to be welcoming and show your potential buyers around the house, showing them the best last. For example, if the kitchen is the best area of the lot, leave that until last when they may be at a stage where they need that final push to help them to decide whether to buy.

Online Profile

Most shoppers search the Internet for a new home, where pictures are king. When it comes to selling a home quickly, you should not publish too few or any unattractive photos or pictures with poor quality - this distracts potential buyers and may turn them away. The images should be of high quality and taken with a 5-megapixel camera or better, and not with a mobile phone. The photos must appeal to the buyer and must prompt them to take an interest in your property. However, be sure that you don't make the photos seem too staged or fake. The photos you take must be well lit and must show the property from different angles that show both the interiors and exteriors.

Choosing to not use a realtor

There are benefits to not using a realtor. For one, you don't have to pay the realtor commission, which can eat up 6% of your profit. Not paying commission allows you to set a lower asking price, which can result in the house selling faster, which as you know, is ideal for house-flipping. If you are worried about selling a house on your own, it isn't as hard as you might think. If you have negotiated for the purchase of your house flip mostly by yourself, you're more than prepared to sell it.

How to price your house?

This is probably the most important step when you're selling your house flip. If you ask for too much, it can take a long time to sell, and you want to ask enough to make a decent profit. The value of a property is determined by factors like number of bedrooms, neighborhood trends, square footage, and upgrades. There are a two main ways to find out what a house is worth.

Comparison

Look at what other similar houses in the area have sold for. Search on sites like zillow.com and homegain.com to compare listings. For houses that have sold recently and are not currently on real estates, you can call a county recorder's office and find out what they sold for. When you're getting closer to listing your house and still working on repairs, be sure to keep an eye on properties selling around you.

A realtor comparative

Even if you aren't using a realtor, you can have one come in and do a comparative market analysis (abbreviated as CMA) for you. Typically, this is a free service, and you get an expert opinion on what your house is worth. A realtor will do an in-depth analysis of similar homes that have sold in the last 3-6 months, and give you a low end and high end of where you should price your house.

Working with the buyer

If you're working without a realtor, you have to be extra careful about buyers. You don't want to accept an offer from a buyer who ends up being unqualified, and starting over from scratch. The key to avoiding this is to require the potential buyer to get pre-approved for a loan. Contact the loaner yourself to be sure if the buyer says they are already pre-qualified. When you're in the closing stages, have a lawyer or title company on your side. You want both yourself and the buyer to have a legal representative present during this final step.

If you have multiple offers on the table, you can use this to your advantage by playing them against each other. Returning to each potential buyer and telling them that you're getting better and better deals means you can increase the offer price and reduce or eliminate any unforeseen costs. Set the date and time when you will receive the best offers. If someone is interested in the property, they will respond in time.

Closing the Deal

The process of closing houses for sellers begins as soon as offers are received. Prepare for negotiations. Even if the offer is made at the asking price, you can always come up with a counteroffer, if there are multiple offers available. You have three options when you receive an offer from the buyer - you can accept the conditions, you can accept it after making some changes, or you can reject the offer.

When you accept an offer, you need to set a completion date and no doubt your legal representative will set this. This will also determine the profit that you make because every month of ownership is another month of costs. If you have borrowed to renovate be quick to pay this back and here, you should know that finance should be on a no penalty basis for early payment.

You must ensure that you and the buyer agree to all the terms of sale and agree to it in writing. You need to have a watertight sale agreement including all the conditions both the parties agree to. Once this document is ready and everything is in order, it is time to seal the deal by signing the documents.

Sign the documents to transfer the file. Make sure that there are no errors. Put simply, the deal is done when the buyer gives the seller money against a title deed. The buyer and the seller must be present at the closing together with their real estate agents, the closing agent and their lawyers, or any other practice that is common in your region.

Chapter 11: How to Properly Calculate a Home's After Repair Value

After you've taken the time to figure out what your budget is going to be for your investment property and have also done some research on your current credit score and how you're going to go about getting a loan for the project you're planning to take on, you can finally begin to think about the next step in the investment property process.

What is the ARV?

ARV is the number almost all investment property professionals use when he or she is attempting to figure out how much their property is going to be worth after they've made their desired renovations. Once this figure is calculated, the investor then knows how much profit he or she can expect to see if the home were to be purchased. This calculated number includes the cost of repairs that are going to need to be made on the property, which is why it is a number that most serious property investment professionals find useful if not essential.

While you can certainly hire a real estate agent who specializes in house flipping to calculate an ARV for you, if you are looking at a lot of properties during your initial search (and you should be), then it's likely that you're going to want to know how to do these calculations yourself. It's important that you do not underestimate the cost that you're going to accrue by implementing repairs on a property.

Calculate the ARV

The following equation is used to after repair value:

ARV= [Retail Value*.7]-Rehab

Let's solve this equation through an example. Let's say that you're interested in a property that has a retail value of $250,000. The house is large, but it needs a significant amount of work. After you do some renovation estimating, you find that your renovation costs are going to be around $60,000. Remember, you're going to want to be as detailed as you can be as you make your initial renovation estimates, and it is also probably a good idea to have your estimates be slightly high rather than slightly low. After you do this math, you find that the ARV is $115,000. What this means is that if everything goes as planned, after you're finished renovating the home, the house should be worth around $365,000. Of course, this is largely going to depend on where the house is located and a variety of other factors that need to be considered, but this example should have been able to provide you with a concrete example of ARV in action. The best advice here is to take your time as you do mathematical research for each property that you may end up purchasing, and if you do find that you're unable to adequately do these calculations on your own, it's always safe to find a realtor who can crunch these numbers for you.

Chapter 12: How to Flip the House Quickly

The most important part of flipping houses in a short period of time so that you can make more profit is learning how to actually do it.

By combining your own best efforts, the effort of your team and excellent business practices, you will be able to make your flips go quicker and smoother. The number one thing that you can do to do this is practice. The more flips that you do, the better you and your team will get at flipping and the faster you will all be able to work on the projects that you have set out to complete.

Be organized. You will not be able to get anywhere with your renovation projects if you are not organized and prepared to make the most out of the project. It is a good idea to have a checklist of everything that you must do when you are looking for the property, renovating the property and selling the property. Being organized will help reduce the amount of time that you would spend preparing to do the project and will help you to do your flips much faster.

As you become more comfortable with your general contractor and the people who are working on the home, you will learn the way that they work and what they are able to do in different amounts of time. Learn how they work and what their strengths are. Encourage them to do the same thing as you and get organized.

The business aspect of investing in homes can take up a lot of your time, but if you do it the right way, you will be able to get the project done much faster. As you get deeper into the business of flipping houses, you will find that you will have more funds to be able to pay people sooner to do the work.

If someone offers you list price on the home, you should absolutely take it. Don't wait for someone to offer above list price because that day may never come and you may end up losing the full list price offer that you just received.

Cash offers are always king when it comes to selling the home. If someone is offering you cash for the home, but they want to pay slightly below the list price, take that offer. Cash deals can be handled faster than their mortgage counterparts, and you will be able to close on the house in a shorter period of time. You may be surprised to find just how many people are willing to offer you cash for the home that you have just flipped.

Your reputation as a business person is so important in the world of investment properties. You need to make sure that people see you as a good flipper and not as someone who rips people off with the houses that you have completed. You could be surprised to find that you will have an easier time selling houses if you have a good reputation than you would if you have continuously ripped people off in the time that you have been in business. Make sure that you know what you are doing when you are renovating the home to help you save time.

Speeding up your flipping

Offer Incentives to your workers

Your general contractor and the crews that they have will work faster if there is something that they are looking forward to at the end of the project. Make sure that the incentives that you offer are not going to cut too much into your budget. If you offer too high of an incentive that costs you too much money, the money that you save on fewer mortgage payments will not be worth it in the end and may end up being much more expensive than if you would have just let the crews finish on time.

Get Your Hands Dirty

It was your idea to flip the home. You likely have, at least, a small amount of experience working in homes or doing some type of renovation or this is not something that you would have chosen. Even if you don't have any experience, anyone is able to tear down old wallpaper, clean up debris or change out light bulbs in all of the rooms throughout the house. Consider getting your own hands dirty to help finish the project more quickly.

By doing all of these things, you will not only be able to speed up the process of getting your home done, but you will also be able to learn more about what it is like to be on the other side of completing a home. Make sure that you do everything that you can while you are doing this so that you will be able to get things done more quickly.

Don't Cut Corners

Saving time by skipping a few steps may seem like a good idea, but it will end up costing you much more time in the long run. When you cut corners on your renovation project, you are risking ruining the entire thing because you were too impatient to wait until it was truly time to unveil the newly renovated house. Don't cut corners to save money, time or for any reason at all. You will end up paying for it at some point during your project.

Combine Steps

There are other steps to your renovation that can be combined, too. If you have the budget to pay for it and really want to speed things up, consider talking to your general contractor about hiring more people on the crew. This will allow them to work in one area of the home while there is another project going on in a different area of the home. By doing this, you will be able to speed the project up, and you can take up to half the time that it would have taken to finish the project.

Benefits of Flipping Quickly

The result of a quicker flipped home will be noticeable and will draw more people in. People who saw the home in its former condition will be interested in what you did and how you did it so quickly.

A home that is flipped more quickly will be able to sell faster, too. This is because it will be completed and will be ready to go back on the market in a shorter period of time than if it was still being renovated and still taking a long time to complete.

Chapter 13: Flipping for the Most Profit

Profit is the name of the game. It's no good just seeing a house that you think looks cheap. You have to see what you can compare it with. You have to see the full extent of the work needed to renovate the house and know that the price you will be able to realize will give you the profit that you anticipated within the time frame decided upon.

Making a plan

A business plan or plan of action serves as a blueprint of the things you intend to accomplish. This is an important first step because this will help keep your business on the right track. It allows you to organize your resources, anticipate problem areas and evaluate the best course of action.

Explore the market

Research diligently for a house located at a strategic area that you can buy at a low price. There are good houses that are sold in the market due to emergency situations, such as transfers of residence or divorces. Be aware, though, that the market varies by state, so take time to do research before signing purchase agreements. Learn the rules and methods of flipping houses that will apply to your target location as these can differ in every state.

Build Relationships with Industry Professionals

A professional team of industry experts will save you more money than anything else you can do, and we're not just talking about construction workers. Although every flipper hopes to turn a house within three to six months, even then, you'll have to pay taxes, loans, insurance, maintenance, utilities, selling costs, and the necessary repairs.

Narrow your choices and inspect them personally

After exploring all the options available, the next thing to do is pick your top choices. It's best to tour your top two or three houses physically, rather than doing so online. There may be areas or aspects that cannot be viewed on a virtual tour.

Keep a notebook with you so you can write down the pros and cons of each of your choices. This will allow you to review the entries later on. Never buy a property that you have not personally visited. The time invested in viewing the unit is always worth it.

Estimate the cost of renovations

Once you've got your eyes set on a house, you need a competent estimator at the onset of your flipping business, unless you're a qualified estimator yourself. The estimator will compute the projected cost of the entire project, including the processing of legal documents, the renovation, and the estimated timeframe it will take to sell the house.

Negotiate to buy the property

Buy the house at the lowest price you can negotiate. It is important to note that the cheapest price may not always be the best, especially if you have to perform major renovations that will put a sizeable hole in your wallet. Be a smart flipper by adding together the total purchase costs of the house and the estimated cost of its renovation. The numbers will help you arrive at a final decision about purchasing the property. This will ensure that the money you give upfront is worth the property you're buying.

Obtain your renovation/building permit from designated institutions

Before you begin with the renovations or remodeling, you must first secure the necessary construction permits.

Neglecting to acquire and display your building permit can be costly. Minor repairs such as replacing a patio or adding built-in cabinets normally don't require permits. However, for major repairs such as room additions, alterations and kitchen remodeling, you will need a building permit.

Make It a Quick Flip

One of the things that will make you the most profit on your flip is to minimize the time from purchase to sale. The longer you hold onto the house; the more money it will cost you. If you have done a good job rehabbing the house and you've staged it well, and several weeks have passed without an offer, it's time to act on what could be holding back the sale. You won't know what's wrong if you haven't been asking your prospects for their opinions. Don't forget to leave a sign-in sheet for buyers who come with a realtor, and go by every few days to collect the cards from visiting agents. Give them a call and ask them for feedback.

Avoid Over-Pricing Your Flip

Don't try to make all your money on one flip. A fair price for a flip will help it to sell faster; a quick sale means more money. If you price a home over what the market will bear, with the mindset that you can always reduce the price if it doesn't sell in a few weeks, you have done yourself a great disservice.

Chapter 14: Common Flipping Mistakes to Avoid

It would be unrealistic to think you won't make mistakes during your first house flip, but you can avoid making the most common mistakes. By anticipating problems that all house-flippers tend to come across, you can be better prepared and less surprised when things become difficult or messy. Here are the missteps to watch out for:

Changing your Budget

Stick to the proposed budget. A common mistake is not having sufficient funds to flip a property. Before you can flip or even purchase a property, you must ensure that you have the necessary financing available to complete the project you will be undertaking. You must always keep your finances in order and also leave some buffer funds for any unforeseen expenses.

Refusing to Seek Outside Help

Investors tend to seek help wherever they can find it, as a coup in the house is a tremendous effort. Do you have a buddy who says he's game if you can invest or fix? Think twice. Flipping a property can be stressful. Therefore, it is a good idea to work with those who are familiar with the process of flipping and know about all the work that's involved therein. If you decide to buddy up with your personal contacts, then ensure that the business relationship doesn't hamper your personal relationship.

Lack of Knowledge

Knowledge is power when it comes to house-flipping. You can avoid bad deals, bad buyers, and more when you have hard facts to fall back on. A common mistake house-flippers make is they don't educate themselves enough. They don't understand the real estate market, which repairs are the most important, or how to market and sell the house. Not knowing enough might not ruin your first house flip, but it can certainly result in you not making as much profit as you could, with a little more education.

Exit Strategy

To make sure that you are successful in your business, you should always work out an "exit strategy" that largely depends on the price at which you listed the house. Contact your broker to determine the price listed, so you can quickly find the price of your home to reduce the time it costs to pay.

You don't have enough money

Too many people dive into house-flipping only to run out of money halfway through, leaving them stuck with a rundown property and little chance at making a profit. To avoid this, don't start a house flip until you are absolutely sure you have enough or can get a loan. If you get a loan, make sure that you can pay it back relatively quickly.

Want to Make All Your Profit on One Flip

The key to consistent flipping success is to flip many medium-priced houses and make a reasonable profit on all of them. Many beginners in the business try to make all their money in one flip, so they go out and buy an expensive house, sink a ton of money in repairs, and end up having it eat into their profits because they need to hold onto it longer than expected. Buying and flipping expensive homes doesn't necessarily mean you'll make more money. What it does mean is that you risk more money to "perhaps" make more profits—perhaps being the operative word.

Don't Have Time to Manage the Flip Properly

Poor management happens when newbies try to flip houses while they continue to work a full-time job. It's possible to flip and work at the same time if you are willing to build your business slower and you are patient with the work. You won't make as much money, but it's a way to keep your sanity and financial freedom. If you do have to work another full-time job while you begin building your house flipping business, don't try to do all the work yourself. The frustration and time spent will probably prove your downfall. Hire a good team of experts to do the job and someone to manage the flip while you work your other job.

Step off the Math

Not sticking to your original plan is the number one mistake flippers make. It's not that they don't know the highest price they can pay and still make a profit; it's usually moving into more expensive repairs that get new flippers into trouble. You just cannot compromise on the math. Commit yourself to making zero adjustments to what you think you can get for the house after the repairs. It's a dangerous game you play when you begin to justify putting more expensive repairs into a home in hopes of getting more for it when you sell.

Using People Whom You Know as Contractors

As much as you possibly can, you should seek to look at flipping homes as a business and not like a recreational side activity that you do in your spare time. Even if you do most of your house flipping on the side when you're first getting started, you should still approach this endeavor as professionally as possible. To this end, it would probably be a good idea to avoid hiring friends or family members as contractors whenever it can be avoided.

Acting as if You Have all the Time in the World

Sure, no one is going to be watching your every move when you're flipping a house to make sure that you're sticking to a strict deadline, but that's what you have to push yourself to do! The reality is that the longer that you're holding onto a property, the more money and effort you're spending on fixing it up. The faster that you can renovate the property and get it up for resale, the quicker you are going to see money re-enter your pocket.

Failure to Appropriately Allocate Funds

One of the biggest mistakes that a new property investor can make is put themselves into a situation where they do not have enough money to complete a project. This type of problem is a result of poor financial planning, and if this happens to you then you are going to have a hard time not only flipping the property, but also getting yourself out from under the debt that you're in.

You go too cheap

After spending a load of money on getting the house, house-flippers are often tempted to go too cheap when it comes to repairs. The last thing you want is for the house to still look like it needs work, because only a certain kind of buyer is willing to take on projects as soon as they move in, and "fixer-upper" houses tend to sell below the asking price. When you're making repairs, don't pick a brand just because it is the cheapest. You don't want to buy the most expensive thing either, but there is a middle ground where you pay for quality. This helps you out in the long run and allows you to sell the house at a good price without having buyers comment on how things look rundown or cheap.

Chapter 15: Why you should have an Exit Strategy When Flipping Houses

An exit strategy can be best defined as a predetermined plan that a property investor puts into place prior to even purchasing a single investment property to flip. The reality is that not all homes are flipped successfully. Some property investors do not anticipate their costs correctly, and they end up actually losing money on the home that they originally purchased in the hope of seeing a profit. This is why an exit plan matters. The exit strategy is going to allow you to keep in mind your final goals in terms of profit and the steps that you'll need to take in order to see the profit that you hope. If you do not purchase your investment property with at least two potential exit strategies in mind, you are making a huge mistake.

Exit Strategies

Putting the Property up for Sale at Your Ideal Asking Price

This first exit strategy can be regarded as every property flipper's ideal scenario. If you were looking to sell your property at a price that would be sure to allow you to walk away with a significant profit, then you would look to use the break-even price in order to figure out what a good profit percentage would be. Ideally, you are obviously going to want to ask a higher asking price than the price that you paid when you sold the property. If you have financially planned correctly and have done sound renovations to your property, then the hope is that you will generate interest in your property based on its new look.

Lower Your Asking Price

Of course, every house flipper's greatest hope is that their home is going to sell at their highest asking price, but unfortunately this is not always the case. Perhaps you've come to find that you did not do enough preliminary research regarding the neighborhood in which you chose to buy your home, or maybe your repair costs were higher than you anticipated so now the asking price is too high. Regardless of your specific situation, the point is that if your property has been on the market for a while and no one has expressed much serious interest in purchasing it, it may be time to lower your asking price. It would be a good idea to calculate before you purchase the property how much you plan to lower it if and when the time comes when you need to do this.

Negotiate a Lease Option

If you happen to find a buyer who wants to purchase your property but does not have the immediate funds to do so, you could also consider offering him or her a lease option instead of immediately lowering the price. To do this, all you have to do is talk to the potential buyer about paying a rent that will go towards the ultimate possession of the home until he or she has saved enough money to purchase the home in full.

Serving as Property Manager

If you're looking for a steady flow of liquidity on a month-to-month basis, it might be a good idea to consider renting out your investment property to tenants.

Cut Your Losses

It may seem outrageous to say that you may find yourself in a position where you have to sell the house at a price that is going to cause you to lose money, but there are plenty of house flippers out there who have indeed experienced this type of situation.

Chapter 16: Tips for success in Flipping Houses

Flipping houses can provide you a tidy profit if you take the time to learn the appropriate steps to become a successful house flipper. The previous chapters have emphasized the need for thorough market research and a hands-on approach. These tips should help further ease your venture:

- Don't overprice. Your price should be competitive with other properties in that area. Compare your prices with that of other similar properties. Your price has to be reasonable - but not excessive.

- Accomplish all necessary paperwork timely and completely. Each and every transaction should be properly documented to avoid unwanted legal issues.

- Become a student of home improvement. Since your business is flipping houses, you will have to learn about home improvement, architecture and design. Grab this opportunity to acquire a new, useful skill.

- Understand the risks involved. Know that there is an element of danger when it comes to flipping houses. When you go into the business without a clear picture of the risks, you can lose big money.

- Sell at the right time. Selling at the right time can dictate the success or failure of your house flipping.

- Get the help of a competent estimator after renovations. You have to know the correct estimation of the value of the house. You can't just name a list price without computing and comparing against the existing prices of houses of the same size and make.

- Consider hiring an attorney. This is vital if you plan to extend the network of your flipping business. The upfront cost of acquiring a lawyer may be costly, but is definitely cheaper and preferable to facing legal battles. When your business booms, you'll need a competent attorney to oversee the legal aspects of your business.

- Form a team of experts or subcontractors. If you plan to stay in this business, you'll have to hire your own team of experts. This will shorten your turn around time and bring in more sales. Make sure though that you keep track of the added costs and price accordingly.

- As with most worthwhile endeavors, one must remain flexible and be ready to modify these tips based on your specific situation. As long as you remain level headed, you will be able to overcome and come out on top.

- Surround yourself with people who are positive and who have got higher goals in life. Their enthusiasm and optimism are bound to rub off on you. If they can do it, so can you.

- Don't be impatient and don't rush into something if you haven't thought it through. You needn't always make a big profit, and quite frankly that's not possible at all times. It is okay to make small profits as well. This will keep you going. Hang around with positive people, and this energy will rub off on you.

- Positive thinking is quite a powerful tool. If you think positive thoughts, the outcome would be positive as well. Trust your gut, and keep a positive mindset. If you firmly believe that your investment will do well, it will prove that the market conditions are favorable.

- You don't necessarily have to follow what others say or do. A successful investor often ignores what others have to say and would do the opposite of what is perceived to be the norm. In real estate investing, it is okay to ignore conventional wisdom.

Conclusion

If you are new to the business of flipping houses, I hope you'll try some of these proven strategies and also share some new ones you pick up along the way.

Flipping houses is a business venture worth seriously considering. It's a huge money earner if you act timely and follow the formula already tried and tested successfully by so many others. Take note that your primary goal is to earn a profit by buying a house at a cut-rate price and later selling it at a premium, after having added value by renovating and remodeling.

If you choose to go into this lucrative business, be aware of the risks that you may encounter. Don't be discouraged easily though, because starting any business involves some risks. With careful planning and a bit of courage, you will be able to surpass the challenges that the business may bring.

With the information in this book, I am confident you can increase your chances of success. Keep this as a handy reference as you take the plunge and become a highly efficient house flipper. The different tips, steps, and information offered in this book will guide you through your journey of getting started with flipping houses and completing your first project.

Please understand that you need to be patient, consistent, and resilient in your efforts. There will be ups and downs. However, remember that it is all a learning experience and you will be able to attain your goals if you just keep going. Motivate yourself, learn about the real estate market, hire a good flipping team, and get started with flipping properties.

Thank You

I would like to thank you from the bottom of my heart for coming along with me on this journey. There are many investing books out there, but you decided to give this one a chance.

If you liked this book, then I need your help!

Please take a moment to leave an honest review for this book. This feedback gives me a good understanding of the kinds of books and topics readers want to read about and it will also give my book more visibility.

Leaving a review takes less than one minute and is much appreciated.